Easy-to-Use Sermon Outline Series

## Sermon Outlines For
# Special Days and Occasions

Sermon helps for every occasion including:

| | |
|---|---|
| New Year | Children's Day |
| Good Friday | Mother's Day |
| Easter | Father's Day |
| Ascension Day | Labor Day |
| Pentecost | Thanksgiving |
| Memorial Day | Christmas |

Watchnight

compiled by

Charles R. Wood

KREGEL PUBLICATIONS
Grand Rapids, Michigan 49503

# *Preface*

One of the most difficult tasks faced by the pastor is selecting his message for the special days which come with demanding regularity as the year passes. Specialized subjects demand specialized treatment, and helps are not always available which take these needs into account.

This book of sermon outlines and helps is especially geared to provide assistance for "special day sermon preparation." The material covers most of the days observed in the greatest number of Protestant churches.

The use of sermon outlines is always problematic. No two men ever have exactly the same style, and it is often unnatural for a man to use another's material. The materials gathered here are designed to be useable. They are of such nature that they can be used "as is," or they may be easily adapted to fit the style and approach of the individual. In many cases, what has been presented here as a sermon outline might be easily adapted into a larger compass of message or even used as a seed thought from which one might develop his own approach.

The outlines contained in this book have been drawn from a large number of sources and a very broad spectrum of men. They were picked, however, because they are logical, Biblical and preachable. Where possible, credits have been given to the originator of the outline. This has not always been possible due to the fact that materials have a way of losing their identity as they are passed along from generation to generation. This editor must take the responsibility for a number of the outlines which are taken from sermons preached to the fine people of two different congregations during thirteen years of ministry.

It is my sincere hope that the materials gathered together and presented here might prove useful to dedicated men as they seek to ". . . preach the Word, be instant in season. . . ."

Charles R. Wood
Grand Rapids, Michigan

3

# *Contents*

**CONTENTS** - Continued

## Textual Index

# Divine Guidance

*"I will guide thee with mine eye."* Psalm 32:8

**Introduction:**

As we begin a new year, we are reminded again of our need for guidance. This passage gives us a beautiful picture of our loving Lord as our Guide.

## I. The Nature Of God's Guidance

There is no compulsion or coercion in it. It is offered to those who seek it and will willingly follow in the way He makes known. A glance of the follower's eye will surely be met by a glance from the Father's eye.

## II. The Negatives Of God's Guidance

God's voice sometimes says, "Not this way." The way He chooses will not always be the easiest or most pleasant for the right way is not always the easy way. The wrong road, however, never led to the right place.

## III. The Positives Of God's Guidance

It is the path of life and truth, the path of confidence for, "He shall guide you into all truth," and God, "will show me the path of life."

## IV. The Understanding Of God's Guidance

A. God's guidance does not contradict the plain teaching of the Word of God.

B. He opens doors in the areas where He wants us to go and closes them when He does not want us to move.

C. His Spirit leads us if we are in close fellowship with Him.

D. We know we are in the right way when three aspects of His guidance coincide or line-up: His Word, His providential leading in circumstance, and the leading of His Spirit.

## V. The Acceptance Of God's Guidance

The earlier we begin to follow God's guidance, the happier our way will be. If we seek His will every step of the way, we will avoid the pitfalls that entrap our brethren on every side.

# In New Pathways

*"And they commanded the people, saying, When ye see the ark of the covenant of the Lord your God, and the priests the Levites bearing it, then ye shall remove from your place, and go after it." Joshua 3:3*

**Introduction:**
We have come on this first Sunday of the new year to a place of new pathways. These words were directions given to the Israelites as they stood looking across into the land of promise — Canaan. Wherever the ark of the covenant led them, they were to follow, even though they had not passed this way before.

**I. We Have Not Passed This Way Before**
This is always the case when we face a new year. Although its experiences may be similar to that which we have already experienced, the sequence and combination of events which face us are totally unknown.

**II. We Do Not Know What Lies Ahead Of Us**
A new year represents a new adventure. For some, there may be the new birth itself, when they will be able to say, "Old things are passed away, behold all things are become new." For others, there will be the new circumstances of school, employment, marriage, etc. For still others, there may be sorrow, serious illness or even death itself.

**III. We Need An Adequate Guide**
To face this new year and its problems and challenges, we need Someone on whom we can depend, Someone to whom we can entrust our very lives. This is true not only for individuals, but also for our nation in this uncertain day of both opportunity and danger. Reduced to its barest fabric, the question we must answer is: Will we walk with God or turn our backs on Him?

God has planned our journey for us, if we only walk in His way for us, keep our eyes on Him and keep our hearts where He can speak to them.

# A Happy New Year Problem

*"Be ye steadfast, unmoveable, always abounding in the work of the Lord." I Corinthians 15:58.*

**Introduction:**
The beginning of the new year is the occasion for new policies in business — why not new programs in life? Here is one which is truly happy:

**I. An Adjusted Life**
Lot failed miserably in adjustment while Abraham grew into closer, blissful relationship with God. The Word would teach us that a well-adjusted Christian is a well-adjusted person.

**II. A Stable Life**
A life that is not always shifting about provides for inner tranquility.

**III. A Fruitful Life**
An abounding life ever follows proper planting and nourishing.

**IV. A Companionate Life**
The fellowship of others along the pathway makes for a higher and more congenial vocation.

**V. A Secure Life**
Allowing God His way in our lives always results in an outcome guaranteed by divine integrity.

# If

*"But this I say, brethren, the time is short." I Corinthians 7:29.*

**Introduction:**
What would you do if you were told that you have just one more year to live? What would be your reaction? Would you change any of the plans you now have?

Here are some of the things you would undoubtedly think about were you faced with this possibility:

I. **The Value Of Time**
Never again would you just "kill time." You would earnestly desire to recover the many wasted hours of past life. You would begin immediately to count out, ration carefully and wisely use the time left.

II. **The Priorities Of Life**
Certain things once important no longer have much meaning - money, cars, possessions, etc. Other things long taken for granted would suddenly become priceless - love of family, everyday provisions of health and strength, etc.

III. **The Use Of That Last Year Of Life**
No two people would react to this situation in the same way. Some would immediately care for all obligations. Others would begin partaking of pleasures long desired but postponed for more convenient times. Still others would be paralyzed by fear and panic.

IV. **The Righting Of Wrongs**
Conscience, so often quieted by the myth of limitless time, would be reawakened, and concern would arise for those who had been wronged in little things as well as large. Most would make some effort to right wrongs.

**Conclusion:**
Faced with the stark reality of one year to live, most of us would make major adjustments in our lives. The truth of the matter is, however, that none of us knows if he has one more day of life much less one more year. Could it be that the changes we would make faced with one more year ought to be made regardless of how much time we have left.

# Be It Resolved

**Introduction:**
What we are going to do with the time that comes after January 1, is an all-important question. Dr. Joseph Parker used to say, "Some minds have no mountain chains running through them. They are all *flat.* "

If we do not from time to time form some definite resolutions, our lives will be devoid of sovereign purpose and therefore fruitless.

Let us take three words of the Apostle Paul in I Corinthians 2:2, ". . . For I determined . . ." and see if we cannot start a mountain chain in our lives.

I. **Determined To Set Christ Ever Before Me**
Psalm 16:8 says, "I have set the Lord always before me: because He is at my right hand, I shall not be moved."

In every place, condition, company, employment, enjoyment, I will say, "Lord, abide here before me." I will *practice the presence of Christ.* That will so revolutionize things that one will be able to say, "I shall not be moved."

II. **Determined To Show Myself Approved Unto God**
This is done through the study of His word (II Timothy 2:15: "Study to show thyself approved unto God, a workman that needeth not to be ashamed, rightly dividing the word of truth.")

The godly man is a man of meditation (Psalm 1:2 & 3). This is the key to real prosperity (Joshua 1:8).

A ship was wrecked; life-boats were leaving. Two sailors rushed back to the sinking ship because they forgot the compass. When we set sail on the unknown sea of a new year, we must be sure we have the compass (Psalm 119:11).

III. **Determined To Take My Place As A Prayer Warrior**
Ephesians 6:18 says, "Praying always with all prayer and supplication in the Spirit, and watching thereunto with all perseverance and supplication for all saints."

The primary need of God's work today is men and women of prayer power. This is even more important than sermons. Satan laughs at our activities when Christians only half pray.

**Conclusion:**
"As for me." Review the above three resolutions.

-K. L. Brooks

**NEW YEAR**

## *Shifting Scenery*

*"The fashion of the world passeth away." I Corinthians 7:31.*

**Introduction:**
The image of the verse is drawn from a shifting scene in a play represented on a stage. Human life, indeed, is a drama, and its conditions and mutations are merely the stage-settings that are ever shifting.

I. **The New Year** is a good time to consider the serious import of living. We must be sure that we are actors in an earnest play that is real.

II. **The New Year** is a good time to discriminate between what is essential and what is stage-setting and scenery.

III. **The New Year** is a good time to play a part fitting to the scenery of the occasion. To repent, to resolve, to renew as the personal need demands.

-S. B. Dunn

# *Lessons from Christ's Triumphal Entry*

Introduction:

There is so much which we might learn from the event of the triumphal entry of Christ into Jerusalem and the events which surrounded it.

Notice at least the following:

I.   Though Disguised And Poor, He Is Yet King Of This World

II.  He Is A Prince Of Peace And His Victories Are By The Weapons Of Peace

III. We Should Gladly Give To His Service Whatever He Has Need Of

IV.  The Lord Can Use Even The Humblest Of His Creatures

V.   Christ Brings Gladness Wherever He Goes

VI.  Christ Encourages Expressions Of One's Inner Joy

VII. Even In The Midst Of Triumph, There Are Sin And Sorrow

VIII. The Moments Of Greatest Triumph Often Precede Moments Of Greatest Trial

IX.  Christ Will Yet Be The King Who Triumphs Over All

# *The Triumphal Entry*

*"Hosanna to the son of David: Blessed is He that cometh in the name of the Lord; Hosanna in the highest." Matthew 21:9.*

**Introduction:**
As we observe the triumph scene at His entry into Jerusalem, there are several important things to observe for our present:

**I.   The Way Must Be Prepared For Jesus**
This was and is done by His disciples. He goes on his triumphant march through the world as we go with and before Him to make His way known. The Spirit of God uses human agencies to spread the word of the King's coming.

**II.  The Way Is A Costly Way**
Garments were and are cast along the way on which He walks. As those who threw their garments then gave of their best so we must throw down in His way that which is our best — possessions, time, talents, the necessities of life and possibly even life itself. Nothing is too costly for the pathway of a King like Jesus.

**III. The Way Must Be A Way Of Beauty**
The highway of salvation along which Jesus walks should not seem a hard, dusty road, but it should be so portrayed by those who walk it with Him that the world will see it as a way of pleasantness and a path of peace.

**IV. The Way Must Be Marked By Enthusiasm**
The people there that day long ago were not afraid to shout. They expressed their emotion in typical outbursts of oriental emotion. They lacked understanding and genuineness in their expression, but still they made the walls reverberate and the hills re-echo with their shouts. How much more should we who know so much more than they rejoice and cause others to hear our joy. This note of joy is often a missing feature of our day.

-James H. Snowden

# *The Kingship of Christ*

*"He hath on His vesture and on His thigh a name written, King of Kings and Lord of Lords." Revelation 19:16.*

**Introduction:**
Palm Sunday is the day of kingship — the Kingship of Christ. Isaiah gives us the promise of a coming Christ. John the Baptist proclaims an approaching Christ. Paul preaches the Gospel of a crucified Christ. John gives us the vision of an enthroned Christ.

Let us take a careful look at that enthroned Christ.

**I. Who Is This One Upon The Throne?**
As we see Him in the manger in Bethlehem, as a child in the Temple, at His baptism in the Jordan or on the cross, He doesn't seem particularly kingly.

**II. Where Is His Throne?**
It is not at all an obvious throne today. We must remember, however, that the greatest kings have sometimes been uncrowned and their kingdoms all but invisible.

**III. Were The Prophecies Incorrect?**
Were those who predicted that Jesus should come as a king incorrect — were they misled or false prophets? Not if we read them carefully:
   A. David said, "A scepter of righteousness is the scepter of thy kingdom." In so saying he indicated his recognition of the fact that there was something infinitely greater than a political kingdom and that Christ would have that kind of kingdom.
   B. The prophets (notably Isaiah) predicted that the king would serve and suffer as well as reign.

**IV. What Evidence Does He Give Of Royalty?**
   A. His amazing, regal self-control.
   B. His constantly active goodness.
   C. His benevolence like a flowing stream.
   D. His might power demonstrated through omnipotence.

## *The Three Crosses at Calvary*

*"And when they were come to the place which is called Calvary, there they crucified Him. . ." Luke 23:33*

**Introduction:**
Of all the times in history when human malice has been displayed, there probably has never been a more graphic display than that made at Calvary on that Friday which we call "good".

I. **The Motives Of Malice**
The fact that Christ was crucified between two male-factors of some magnitude causes us to wonder just what would motivate the rulers to act thus. There are two suggestions offered:
A. To make His death seem as offensive and odious as possible.
B. To thus brand Him as a great criminal.

II. **The Results Of Malice**
Most of the results of their malice were unseen to them. They included:
A. The cross became a tribunal, foreshadowing the scene at the Day of Judgment. (Note the Judge in the center with a sinner on each side: one is penitent, the other impenitent.)
B. A malefactor became an open witness to Christ's mighty, redeeming love.

III. **The Lessons Of Malice**
There are some things which we may draw from the three crosses of Calvary.
A. The same cross both attracts and repels.
B. The most hopeless may obtain mercy.
C. One may be ever so near mercy and still miss it.
D. The wrath of men is used by God to His own praise. Even the malice demonstrated at Calvary provided God's grace an opportunity to operate.

# The Seven Words from the Cross

**Introduction:**
We may well believe that all of our Lord's words as He hung upon the cross have been preserved. In a very wonderful way the seven utterances that have come down to us represent the seven most important phases of Christ's character and work.

## I. The Word Of Forgiveness
*"Father, forgive them; for they know not what they do."*
*Luke 23:34.*
The Word of Forgiveness. This was probably spoken as the cross, with Christ nailed to it, was lifted up and planted in the ground, with a rough shock of indescribable agony. He hastened to apply the first outgushing of that redeeming blood. His coming to earth was that He might prove God's readiness to forgive men, and now He includes in that readiness even His murderers, the harsh soldiers, Annas, Caiaphas, Herod, Pilate, and all men everywhere.

## II. The Word Of Salvation
*"Today shalt thou be with me in Paradise"* *Luke 23:43.*
The Word of Salvation was spoken about noon. One of the robbers, moved by Christ's bearing and words of tender forgiveness, and perhaps having some previous knowledge of Him, rebuked the railing of the other robber and begged for Christ's help into eternal happiness. How ready was Christ to grant it! He had come for that one thing, to seek and save the lost.

## III. The Word Of Love
*"Woman, behold thy son . . . behold thy mother."* *John 19:26,27*
The Word of Love. Joseph, judging from the silence of the record, may have died long before, and Mary was a widow. Some have held that Christ addressed Mary respectfully but vaguely as "Woman," because had He called her "Mother" she would have been exposed to the rough taunts of the brutal soldiers. Others see in the

words, "And from that hour the disciple took her unto his own home," an indication of Christ's desire that Mary should at once be led away by John and spared the further agony of watching Him. John's devotion to his dying Lord — exposed to the peril of the cross—is thus abundantly recompensed. As John's was the greatest personal love it was honored with the largest earthly requital. earthly requital.

## IV. The Word Of Atonement

*"My God, my God, why hast thou forsaken me?" Matt. 27:46.*

The Word of Atonement, wherein the Son of God entered the deepest pit of human woe, the sense of abandonment and utter loss, and thus became completely at one with our humanity. It was spoken toward the end of that mysterious darkness that seized the country from noon till three o'clock. The divine horror of that moment is unfathomable by human soul. It was blackness of darkness. And yet He would believe. Yet He would hold fast. God was His God yet. My God — and in the cry came forth victory.

## V. The Word Of Physical Suffering

*"I thirst." John 19:28.*

The Word of Physical Suffering, as the fourth was the word of spiritual suffering. Christ's thirst must have been torturing, His body exposed, almost uncovered, to the fierce noonday heat of Palestine. There is no agony like that of unassuaged thirst; it is the one cry of the wounded as they lie untended on the battlefield: "Water! Water!" He thirsts that we may not thirst, that we may receive from Him that gift of the water of life which shall cause us never to thirst any more.

The Scriptures fulfilled in this cry are Psa. 22:15; 69:21. Only when all else had been attended to ("Knowing that all things are finished") did Christ attend to His own physical sensations. They filled a sponge because a cup was impracticable and put it around a stalk of hyssop and thus applied the restorative to His mouth. All that was requisite was a reed two or three feet long, as the crucified was only slightly elevated. He had refused the stupefying draught which would have clouded his facul-

18

ties; He accepts what will revive them for the effort of a willing surrender of His life.

## VI. The Word Of Triumph

*"It is finished." John 19:30.*

The Word of Triumph. This is one word in the Greek and it has been called, "the greatest single word ever uttered." No other man, since the world began, could have said that word as Jesus said it. He had lived a perfect, complete human life in which there were no mistakes, no omissions, no short-comings. The atonement was complete because it was the offering of a perfect life. In one sense nothing He did was ended, but the atoning sacrifice had been offered once for all. Our Lord saw a long wake of light crossing the past and stretching forward to the future.

## VII. The Word Of Reunion

*"Father, into thy hands I commend my spirit." Luke 23:46.*

The Word of Reunion was spoken at 3 p.m., the time of the evening sacrifice. The last act of our Lord in thus commending His spirit to the Father was only a summing up of what He had been doing all His life. He had been offering this sacrifice of Himself all the years. The thought of the Father penetrated and possessed our Lord's whole life. What wonder that He turned to the Father at the last with perfect confidence?

## *Our Lord's Farewell to the World*

### Matthew 26:29

**Introduction:**
Our Lord made a very striking statement to the disciples when He was with them at the table observing the last supper. He said, "I will not drink henceforth of this fruit of the vine, until that day when I drink it new with you in my Father's kingdom." Let us observe what our Lord is expressing:

I. **His Renunciation Of The Joys And Comforts Of Life**
From that moment on He will not partake of these things because He now has other work to do and His compassionate love of mankind constrained Him to be about it.

II. **His Farewell To Earth**
He did not live as an ascetic and He does not die as one. There is no repining. He puts away the cup with as cheerful an air as He took it up.

III. **His Dying Anticipation**
He looked for brighter days, fairer banquets, fresher wine. He was either referring to the second coming and the establishment of His kingdom or to the joys of heaven. In either case, these are great words. If He has reference to the second coming, He is speaking of a time when the glorious wine-cup of the New Jerusalem's best wine shall be passed from lip to lip. If the reference is to heaven, then He speaks of the fact that the joys of heaven are social, and it is a place where He is happy and happy with His people.

Adapted from C. H. Spurgeon

# *The Substitution of Christ*

*(The following is an interesting and suggestive word study which clearly demonstrates the greatness of the work of Christ. It is suitable for adaptation to sermonic form or for use in a sermon.)*

**Introduction:**

The Apostle Paul, in writing to the Church at Corinth, said, "I will very gladly spend and be spent for you." II Corinthians 12:15. The preposition *huper*, translated *for*, is the one Paul uses, and it is applied to Christ as the One who was not only willing, but who did "spend" and was "spent out" (II Corinthians 12:15 R.V.) in acting on our behalf. The word means "bending over to protect" (as a mother bird over her young even to the sacrifice of her life); "service rendered on behalf of another" thus acting in his stead as when the priest offered "sacrifices *for* sins" on behalf of another (Hebrews 5:1). The following will illustrate how faithfully and fully Christ acted on behalf of those who believe in Him. The preposition *huper* occurs in each case and is rendered "for".

**Christ as Giver.** "Given *for* you" (Luke 22:19; I Cor. 11: 24).

**Christ as Atoner.** "Shed *for* you" (Luke 22:20).

**Christ as the Bread.** "Bread . . . *for* the life of the world" (John 6:51).

**Christ as the Good Shepherd.** "Good Shepherd giveth His life *for* the sheep" (John 10:11).

**Christ as the Volunteer.** "I lay down my life *for* the sheep" (John 10:15).

**Christ as the Provision** for ungodly ones and sinners. "Christ died *for* the ungodly" (Rom. 5:6); "Christ died *for* us" (Romans 5:8).

**Christ as the Passover.** "Christ our Passover . . . sacrificed *for* us"(I Cor. 5.7).

**Christ as the Fulfiller of Scripture.** "Christ died *for* our sins according to the Scriptures" (I Cor. 15:3).

**Christ as the Sin-bearer.** "He hath made Him to be sin *for* us" (II Corinthians 5:21).

**Christ as the Deliverer.** "Gave Himself *for* our sins, that He might deliver" (Gal. 1:4).

**Christ as the Substitute.** "Gave Himself *for* me" (Gal. 2:20).

**Christ as the Curse-bearer.** "Made a curse *for* us" (Gal. 3:13).

**Christ as the Burnt-offering.** "Himself *for* us, an offering and a sacrifice to God for a sweet-smelling savour" (Eph. 5:2).

**Christ as the Lover.** "Loved. . . .gave Himself *for* it" (Ephesians 5:25).

**Christ as the Saviour.** "Salvation through our Lord Jesus Christ, who died *for* us" (I Thess. 5:9, 10, R.V.).

**Christ as the Ransom.** "A Ransom *for* all" (I Tim. 2:6).

**Christ as the Redeemer.** "Gave Himself *for* us, that He might redeem us," (Titus 2:14).

**Christ as the Kinsman.** "Taste death *for* every man" (Hebrews 2:9).

**Christ as the Sacrifice.** "Sacrifice *for* sins" (Heb. 10:12).

**Christ as the Sufferer.** "Suffered *for* us" ( Peter 2:21).

**Christ as the Reconciler.** "Just *for* the unjust, that He might bring us to God" (I Peter 3:18).

**Christ as the Example.** "Christ hath suffered *for* us. . . . likewise," etc. (I Peter 4:1).

**Christ as the Inspirer.** "He laid down His life *for* us; and we ought . . ."(I John 3:16).

S.R. Briggs

# The Sight at the Cross

Matt. 27:26, 33-51

**Introduction:**
There are intriguing words in verse 36, "And sitting down, they watched Him there." As they sat down and watched, what did they see?

I. **The Person At The Cross**
   A. Crucifixion common enough in those days that it was not something distinctive in itself.
   B. There were distinguishing factors though:
      1. The refusal of sedation.
      2. The excessive physical punishment.
      3. The prophetic superscription.
      4. The reaction of nature.
      5. The rent in the veil of the Temple.
   C. This man is identified by the very mocking of the throng (the wrath of man praises God even here).

II. **The Event At The Cross**
   A. The culmination of history.
      1. The promise to Adam and Eve (Genesis 3:15).
      2. The call of Abraham (Genesis 12: 1-3)
      3. The establishment of Israel (the nation was "cradle of a king").
      4. All religious symbols and rites.
      5. All of prophecy up until that time.
   B. The focal point of subsequent history.
   C. The dividing line in spiritual experience. In Paul the cross becomes the center, and the position of a man is decided by the side of the cross on which he stands.

III. **The Victory At The Cross**
   A. Satan's claims were paid.
   B. Christ's sufferings were ended.
   C. Man's suffering was ended in Christ.

## IV. The People At The Cross

We now come back to verse 36. Who were they who sat and watched Him there?

A. The common people with their mocking scorn.
B. The religious leaders with their blasphemous scorn.
C. The thieves with the doubting scorn of one.
D. The women with their fearful devotion.
E. The Roman soldiery.
    1. Before the crucifixion worse than all the others.
    2. Afterward subdued by recognition.


**EASTER**

# *The Risen Lord*

*"The Lord is risen indeed"* Luke 24:34

**Introduction:**

This is the day when all voices proclaim, "He is risen." He was buried, but He arose by the mighty power of God, and death is now swallowed up in His victory.

## I. The Object Of The Resurrection

A. For our justification (Romans 4:25).
B. That we might be counted worthy of eternal life (John 10:10; 11:25, 26).

## II. The Result Of The Resurrection

A. The believer is risen with Him (Colossians 2:12).
B. The believer is begotten again to a lively hope (I Peter 1:3-5).

## III. The Demand Of The Resurrection

A. A consecrated life (Romans 6:14, 11:14).
B. That we be in the world but not of it (John 17:11, 16, 19; Colossians 3:1-4).
    1. A worthy walk (Colossians 1:10; 11; 2:6, 7).
    2. Living unto Christ (II Corinthians 5:15 & 17).
    3. Realization of the power of His resurrection (Philippians 3:9-14; I Peter 3:21).

# Christ — The Resurrection and the Life

*"I am the resurrection and the life. . ." John 11:25, 26.*

Introduction:
The death and resurrection of Christ are the two grand fundamental facts on which the whole of Christianity rests. Hence, says the apostle, "If Christ be not risen, then is our faith vain . . ."

What evidences have we that these events really took place?
A. They were public events.
B. They were seen by a great number of persons.
C. They were written down in a book at the time.
D. Monuments, to commemorate those events, were erected — *The Lord's Day* and *The Lord's Supper.*

In addition to the great miracle of Christ's resurrection, similar miracles were wrought both by the Apostles and the Saviour Himself. One of the most interesting of these, and one that excited the greatest attention was the resurrection of Lazarus.

Come with me to the home of Lazarus, and let us observe:

I. **The Facts Stated**
"I am the resurrection and the life."

"I am the author and cause of the resurrection — It so depends on me that it may be said that I am the resurrection itself." This is a strong mode of expression and is often used. He is said to be made unto us Wisdom, Righteousness, Sanctification and Redemption.

II. **The Promise**
There is scarcely, in the whole compass of Revelation, a more beautiful and comprehensive promise than this. Notice — :
A. *The persons to whom it applies.* "Whosoever believeth."

25

B. *The nature of the promise.*
  1. The dead shall live. It would seem that this has reference to those in a state of physical death. He who believed and is now in the grave, though his body moulders there, shall be restored. Jesus illustrated this in the case of Lazarus.
  2. The living shall never die. To the believer, the curse is removed, and the last hour is an *hour of victory* — of *glorious triumph!*

## III. The Appeal
"Believest thou this?"

Let me apply this on a little wider scale than, perhaps, was intended in the text.
A. *To the penitent.* — You are anxious to obtain pardon; you feel you must be pardoned or die. Listen to what is addressed to you in Isa. 1:18; Jer. 31:34; II Cor. 5:19. "Believest thou this?"
B. *To the doubting soul.* — You are not quite sure that your sins are forgiven. You want to hear the voice of God — to know that your name is in the Book of Life. You want the witness of the Spirit. This is a privilege given upon believing — (Acts 15:8; I John 5:19) as our evidence of adoption (Rom. 8:16) and as an evidence of Christ in you (I John 3:24), an evidence of God in you (I John 4:13). "Believest thou this?"
C. *To believers.*
  1. It is your duty to strive to be free from sin, to be like Christ and to love God with all your heart. This is promised (Ezek. 36:25; Jer. 33:8; I Thess. 5:23; Col. 2:10). "Believest thou this?" What is your answer? "Believest thou this?" this?"
  2. God has engaged to provide you with every necessary temporal blessing: Psa. 37:28; Matt. 10:30, etc. "Believest thou this?"
  3. There is a glorious heaven provided for you and promised to you.

Pulpit Aids

# Love at Eastertime

*"And when the sabbath was past, Mary Magdalene, and Mary the mother of James, and Salome had bought sweet spices that they might come and anoint Him."Mark 16:1-6.*

**Introduction:**
The events of Good Friday clearly demonstrated the love of God and that of the Lord Jesus Christ. In the cleared atmosphere of Easter, may we see our obligation to respond to the love of God in Christ. The women who came to the tomb can teach a number of lessons about such love.

I. **True Love Leads To Action**
   A. Love led these women to seek Jesus that morning. Some of them were the last at the cross and the first at the grave.
   B. Love led these women to bring the expensive gift of sweet spices. This shows how true love willingly makes heavy sacrifices.

II. **The Love Leads One To Seek Jesus Early**
The Scriptures make a point of telling us that the women came early in the morning. This teaches us the time to seek the Lord if we love Him.
   A. Early in life (Proverbs 8:17; Ecclesiastes 12:1).
   B. Early in the day (Psalms 55:17). This allows one to be with Him when the mind is fresh and bright.
   C. In the first stages of everything. Not after the circumstances, etc., have piled up to the point of desperation.

III. **True Love Often Faces Difficulties**
The women faced the stone rolled across the mouth of the tomb (at least they thought they did).
   A. The penitent often faces ignorance, unbelief and scoffing friends.
   B. The believer faces the world, doubts, the flesh, etc.
   C. The church faces division and want of harmony, pride, worldliness, indifference, etc.

When there is true love, there will be obstacles to its expression.

IV. **True Love Presses On**

The women could have failed to go because they knew they would face soldiers, a stone and a seal. They refused to be deterred by what they were sure would be difficult. When there is true love, it will push on through the obstacles.

V. **True Love Finds Its Rewards**

Those who press forward in spite of difficulty always find more than they had anticipated.

A. The women sought the dead body of Jesus and found and angel and a living Saviour.

B. Earnest seekers always find more than what they thought they were seeking.

# The Resurrection of Christ

*"Why seek ye the living among the dead?" Luke 24:5*

**Introduction:**

The love with which the Saviour inspired the hearts of His disciples, especially the hearts of the meek women that followed Him, was not quenched by the many waters of His passion and death. Let us journey to behold the place where they laid Him. Let us consider, first, the evidences and, second, the purposes of the second life of Jesus, the life after the resurrection.

I. The Evidences Of Christ's Resurrection
   A. External evidence.
      1. Jesus actually died. A million and one half awe-struck witnesses saw Him die.
      2. Jesus actually was buried. Internment is not always granted to crucified criminals, but providence overruled the sordidness of the cautious Scribes and Pharisees in order to multiply the witnesses to the resurrection.
      3. The sepulchre was somehow emptied on the third day. There are two theories as to how this came to pass.
         a. The rulers said that the body was stolen out of it. It is manifest that the enemies of Jesus would not have stolen it. The idea that the disciples could have done it is improbable at best. It would have been twelve (actually eleven) frightened men against an armed guard of sixty in a city filled with an excited crowd.
         b. The disciples said that the body had risen from it, and this is the position to which the honest inquirer is driven by the evidence.
   B. Internal evidence.
      1. Consider the persecution borne by the disciples that arose out of the disciples determination to witness to the resurrection.

2. Consider the continual failure of the enemies of Jesus to produce the body when such a move would have finally ended the controversy.

## II. The Purposes Of The Resurrection

The resurrection should work out its purposes in our lives.

A. It is a manifestation, a vindication of ancient prophecy and of the personal character of the Messiah as well.

B. It is a seal of the acceptance of the sacrifice of Jesus, and by consequence of that, it is of infinite moment to confirm the hopes of the world.

C. It is an earnest of our own rising, a pledge of immortality for the race for which the Second Adam died.

D. It is a great encouragement. There is great error in Christendom today, and that is in the direction of believing in a dead Christ. He is not dead; He is living — living to listen to prayer and to forgive sin.

W. M. Punshon

# *The Resurrection*

*(The following is a sermonic analysis of the entire fifteenth chapter of I Corinthians with special attention to the way in which it all clusters around the resurrection.)*

**Introduction:**
In a time like this, we need assurance regarding eternity. Such assurance is possible and comes from a passage such as this.

I. **The Importance Of The Resurrection (1-4)**
   A. Has wide prominence in Scripture.
   B. Is a focal point of the eternal conflict between Christ and Satan.
   C. Is a subject of historical enquiry and proof.

II. **The Assurance Of The Resurrection (20-23)**
   A. The principle of the first-fruits. The very first grain was brought to the Lord to symbolize that the entire harvest belonged to Him and also that He would receive His required tithe.
   B. The purchase of life. Christ bought life and brought immortality to light at Easter.

III. **The Method Of The Resurrection (35-38; 42-44)**
   A. The illustration from nature: seed must die to grow, and the final product is quite different from what was originally planted.
   B. The resurrection body will be a different one. It will be spiritual rather than physical.

IV. **The Meaning Of The Resurrection (54-57)**
   A. The power and strength of death is broken. Death and the grave have forever lost their finality.
   B. The pathway to victory is opened up through the Lord Jesus Christ.

## *Something New for Easter*

*"If any man be in Christ . . . a new creature. . . ." II Corinthians 5:17*

### Introduction:
We make a big thing out of new belongings for Easter. Everyone wants a new hat, coat, etc. These desired things are merely temporal and pass away. God wants us to have something new and lasting. God wants us to have a new heart for Easter.

### I. The Old Creation
This is the reason why we need something new for Easter. The natural man is:
A. Possessed of a sinful nature and an evil heart.
B. Alienated from God.
C. Stuck with a low set of values and standards arising out of a distorted mind.
D. Possessed of a stilted and stunted life. He is unhappy, purposeless and doomed. The inner man controls the outer man and makes things a real mess.

### II. The New Creation
A. The new man has a new nature and a new heart.
B. The new man is in fellowship with God.
C. The new man has a high set of values arising out of the revealed Word of God to understand and obey.
D. The new man has a new life.

### III. The Re-Creation
A. The change is effected as the result of a relationship. The verse says "in Christ" meaning that He must be accepted as Saviour and the individual must be related to Him.
B. The change is open to all. It says, "if any man", and inclusion or exclusion is left up to the individual.
C. The change is readily available. It is a matter of a man accepting what Christ has offered.

# *Easter Peace*

*"Peace be unto you." John 20:19.*

**Introduction:**
These were the first words of the first Easter sermon. They were spoken to those who gathered on the evening of that first Easter day. They have brought to those who heard them a fourfold peace.

I.  **Peace Concerning Jesus**
Of course they had been distressed concerning Jesus. They had expected much of Him, and He had permitted Himself to be slain. There came the troubles of Easter when it had been reported that His body was no longer in the tomb. The situation grew complicated. A few of them gathered together to discuss the happening and, perhaps, make their own plans for the future. Then He appeared in the midst saying, "Peace be unto you." Now they knew that all was well concerning Jesus.

II.  **Peace Concerning Themselves**
They had been much excited about themselves. Since He had urged them to "follow Him," they had done little else. They had heard His mightiest words and seen His mightiest works, and they had dreamed of empires. Now, all had been changed.

They remembered that He had tried to prepare them for disappointment. Surely He had pointed out to them the shadow of the cross. It looked as if they might have to go back to the boats of fishermen. Then He came.

"The path they had lost in the depths of Gethsemane had been found again on the heights of that splendid Easter evening, in the word and presence of the Lord Himself, and it had led them back into Galilee, and thence into all the world, in the highest service ever given to men. And thus finding Jesus they found themselves."

III. **Peace Concerning Fear Of The Jews**
Would those who had crucified the Master deal less harshly with the disciples?

"The disciples shut the doors, therefore, 'for fear of the Jews' when they called their solemn assembly on that first Easter evening. But on through closed doors, past possible sentinel and into their very midst came Jesus, speaking away their fears and saying, "Peace be unto you." Thrown on the defensive, the Jews were now in so great fear for their own lives that the disciples were in no further danger from them. And so, with Jesus on his side, the believer ever dwells in safety of body and soul, for the Lord will deliver him from all his foes."

## IV. Peace Concerning Pardon From Sin

Sin had come into the world to destroy the world, but Christ had come to destroy sin, and when the great atonement was made on Calvary, salvation was thereby secured for all believers.

"The first word of Jesus, therefore, to His disciples was a word of peace and pardon from sin. Henceforth peace on earth and good will toward men were possible because there was peace with God. When nations believe in God and trust in Him, there is peace; when they despise and reject Him, there is war. It has always been so and always will. The nations have forgotton God now, and He has left them to their own wicked devices to show them how helpless they are without Him. But they have brought upon themselves the strife, bloodshed and heartache of universal warfare and can blame no one for it but themselves, for in their very midst, especially at this holy Easter time, stands the Son of God pleading with them and saying, "I would but ye would not. . .peace be unto you. . .my peace I give unto you."

E. A. Repass

# The Fact of the Resurrection

*"He is not here: for He is risen, as He said."* Matthew 28:6

**Introduction:**
The scene painted in the Scriptures of that first Easter morning is one of dazzling beauty. There are few scenes in Scripture or history which can rival the majesty of that morning.

I. **The Deluded Objections**
   A. Some say that miracles are impossible.
   B. All face the fact that history must be explained. Attempts are:
      1. That Christ swooned and later revived and escaped the tomb.
      2. The disciples stole the body.
      3. The disciples (and all His followers) had hallucinations.

II. **The Excellent Witnesses**
   A. All the above objections are answered when we realize that the disciples staked their very lives and witness on the fact of the resurrection.
   B. The objections were never answered in their day. It would have ended Christianity almost before it could begin.

III. **The Wondrous Fact**
   A. The resurrection is a well attested historical fact.
   B. The Christian faith thus stands as logical and reasonable for it is attested by historical fact.

IV. **The Glorious Meaning**
   A. The authentification of Christ. The resurrection demonstrated the truth of His predictions and the authority of His work.
   B. The defeat of Satan. His power and dominion were broken, and the purposes of God were vindicated.
   C. The empowerment of the saints. Real life became possible with real power for its living. "Because I live, ye shall live also."

# *The Ascension*

*"Ye men of Galilee, why stand ye gazing up into heaven? this same Jesus, which is taken up from you into heaven, shall so come in like manner as ye have seen Him go into heaven."*
*Acts 1:11*

I. **The Occasion Of The Message**
Jesus had done His great work. The manger, the cross, the tomb were all things of the past. Now the last act takes place. The disciples are assembled around Him. The great Bishop gives His last charge, the loving friend His final promise, the Divine Master His last commission, God-incarnate His last benediction. We conceive at this moment a solemn silence prevails; every heart is awe-striken as Jesus slowly rises from their midst. No hand can touch Him; no voice can entreat His stay. He rises higher, they see His smile, the cloud hides Him.

II. **The Import Of The Message**
   A. Christ Jesus, the God-man, the tender friend, the gracious benefactor, "this same Jesus," shall come again. We shall see Him more exalted but not less gracious or familiar when He comes back.
   B. As He ascended without signifying the time beforehand, so He will descend suddenly, in presence of spectators, the conveyance a cloud. Then it was as a man's hand for size compared with what it shall be; for when He comes He will bring ten thousand of His saints with Him.

III. **The Purpose Of The Message**
   A. *To rebuke.* "Ye men of Galilee." Your Lord has been your companion, but remember, He is none the less your Lord. Do as He bids. "Why stand ye gazing," so disconsolately? Did He not say, "I will not leave you orphans?"
   B. *To comfort.* No words could be more calculated to do this. Picture the group as they look on one

36

another. Does not Thomas think of his unbelief? Peter of the denial, the sleeping in Gethsemane, the absence from the cross? John of the time when "they all forsook Him," as well as of the last supper, and ten thousand other scenes which illustrated their folly and His loving-kindness?

C. *To stimulate* them in their work.

-Stems and Twigs

# Fourteen Appearings of Christ after His Resurrection

**Introduction:**

There are no less than *fourteen* recorded appearings of Christ before Paul wrote to the Church of Corinth, and fifteen if we include Christ's manifestation to John in the Isle of Patmos. The fourteen appearings are as follows:—

A. To Mary Magdalene (John 20:14; Mark 16:9).
B. To the other women (Matt. 28:9).
C. To Peter (ICor. 15:5; Luke 24:34).
D. To the two disciples on their way to Emmaus (Mark 16:12, 13; Luke 24:13-32).
E. The day He appeared to the disciples, in the absence of Thomas (John 20:19-24).
F. To the disciples when Thomas was present (John 20:24-29).
G. In Galilee, at the sea of Tiberias, to Peter, John, Thomas, James, Nathanael, and two others (John 21:1-14).
H. To the disciples on a mount in Galilee (Matt. 28:16).
I. To more than five hundred brethren at once (I Cor. 15:6).
J. To James the apostle (I Cor. 15:7).
K. To all the apostles assembled together (I Cor. 15:7).
L. To all the apostles at His ascension (Luke 24:50, 51; Acts 1:9, 10).
M. To Stephen, when he was being stoned to death (Acts 7:56).
N. To Paul (I Cor. 15:8; Acts 9:3-5; 22:6-10).

Such a mass of evidence attesting any given fact would be accepted as proof positive as to its validity in any court of justice.

-S. R. Briggs

# *This Nation Under God*

**Introduction:**
Memorial Day is a significant and valuable day of national observance. It is wise to look back not only to remember but also to learn.

## I. See The Hand Of God On Our Nation
A. Wars have been few and blessings many.
B. This is true because this is a nation founded on God and the Bible.
C. Many of the men who founded this nation had an eye for the Word of God and a heart for the Lord.

## II. Learn The Lessons Of Caution
A. God's goodness sometimes becomes a matter of pride.
B. People in the past have forgotten that God was the One who accomplished for them, and they paid dearly.
C. We must have more than a head-nodding, indifferent assent concerning the part God has played in making this a great nation.

## III. Learn The Lessons Of Gratitude
A. "Righteousness exalteth a nation, but sin is a reproach to any people."
B. God still demands obedience to His moral law as a demonstration of man's gratitude to Him.
C. God also demands faith as a demonstration of gratitude.

## IV. See The Importance Of The Matter
A. We trust that "these dead shall not have died in vain."
B. The test of whether or not their death has been in vain will be in whether or not we keep our liberty in the years ahead. If we lose our freedom, they will have died in vain.
C. A nation which honors God will know His blessing. A nation disobedient will know the carnage of His judgment.

# *Watch!!!*

## Matt. 26:41

**Introduction:**
The Lord Jesus wants all His boys and girls to live lives that are pleasing to Him. This isn't always easy to do. If we are going to please Him, we are going to have to watch certain things.

**I.   Watch Yourself**
This is very important, and you will have just about all you can handle if you keep yourself under control.

**II.  Watch Your Eyes**
Be sure they look upon the good and pure things and also see the needs of poor people.

**III. Watch Your Nose**
Keep it going in the right direction and don't let it get to snooping and prying around the business of other people.

**IV. Watch Your Mouth**
Be sure that nothing unclean enters and that nothing impure comes out.

**V.  Watch Your Tongue**
See that it doesn't speak unkind words but rather is used to praise and honor God and to teach others the Gospel.

**VI. Watch Your Hands**
See to it that they don't steal or just lie idle.

**VII. Watch Your Feet**
See to it that they do not lead you into evil places but that they walk in the pathway of duty and the highway of holiness.

**VIII. Watch Your Temper**
Ask God to help you control it and make it like the Lord Jesus.

# *Idolatry*

*"Little children keep yourselves from idols"* (I John 5:21)

**Introduction:**

An idol is a heathen god. In the second commandment it is called a "graven image." Men bow down to idols and serve them.

These idols are:—

1. The works of human handicraft.
2. They are foolish.
3. They are helpless.
4. They are hideous.
5. They are hurtful.

It is  possible even for children to make such "idols" of certain things that they will be kept from God Who deserves their best thoughts and affections and services, Who claims the bloom and dew of their days.

I. **Idol Self**

This love of self is born in us and if not early checked, will be our master. It tempts one to falsehood, to unkindness, to greediness and to pride for it feeds upon these. You must gratify it at whatever cost, and then it often demands more than you can obtain for it. Self is a dreadful idol. Beware of it.

II. **Idol Dress**

We all like bright expensive clothes, but there is danger on the other side — danger of thinking more of the "outward adorning" than of those hidden ornaments of neatness and quietness which are so priceless in God's esteem. You may forget the pearl in anxiety about its setting. Fashion is a perilous boat for you to venture in, and before you are aware it may wreck you.

III. **Idol Food**

It cannot be denied that children may be so fond of nice

things, so fond of the things of the table, that these things are their idols. They dream of things and want them and are angry when they connot have their desires The wholesome things are despised because they are plain.

## IV. Idol Pleasure

Do not children desire exciting amusements until they are miserable without them? We have known children whose Sundays were a "weariness" to them and their studies a positive punishment. That should not be so. Their pleasures were their idols. Now you are exhorted to keep yourselves from them.

## V. Idol Conquest

A. You can implore from above daily assistance against them.

B. Be vigilant against them.

C. Be self-denying. This is a capital cure for these idols. If you can "deny yourself" you have the secret of victory over these idols.

D. Yield your heart to God. You have not two hearts; therefore if God has your heart, these idols cannot have it. Endeavor to occupy it for God, to present it to God continually, to view it as consecrated to God. Implore the Saviour to dwell in it by His Holy Spirit, and with Him reigning there all "idols" will be banished — you shall be kept from them, though you are but a "little child."

-Outline Sermons for Children

# The Eulogy of a Mother

## Proverbs 31:10-31

**Introduction:**
Most can conjur up a memory of mother. The older mother is, the more likely the picture is really satisfying. Whatever yours was like, however, the Bible paints a picture of an ideal mother. This was written in another age, but the principles were the same then and now.

I. The Worth Of The Ideal Mother (verse 10)
   A. This is, unfortunately, not the picture of a "typical" woman, then or now.
   B. Her worth is tied to her rarity.

II. The Character Of The Ideal Mother (11-19)
   A. She is trustworthy.
   B. She is industrious.
      1. She is willingly working.
      2. She places the comfort of her household above her own.
      3. She is strong in her ways.
   C. She is a good provider.
      1. For others.
      2. For her own household.
      3. For herself.

III. The Effect Of The Ideal Mother (23-27)
   A. Her husband's welfare is promoted.
   B. She has personal peace without fear of the future.
   C. Her family prospers under her guidance.

IV. The Reward Of The Ideal Mother (28-31)
   A. She receives the praise of her family.
   B. She gets to partake of the fruits of her own labor.

V. The Secret Of The Ideal Mother (30)
   A. She is not typical.
   B. The pathway of her greatness lies through her recognition of spiritual values.". . .the fear of the Lord. . ."

# "Carte Blanche"

*"Then Jesus answered and said unto her, O woman, great is thy faith: be it unto thee even as thou wilt." Matthew 15:28*

**Introduction:**

In these words our Saviour gave this woman a "blank check" and told her to fill in the amount she needed. That was how much her faith impressed Him. Such a "blank check" is known as "carte blanche"

I. **What Was It's Extent?**
   A. Far enough to baffle the powers of hell.
   B. Far enough to heal her daughter completely.
   C. Far enough to bring a blessing immediately.
   D. Far enough to allow her to partake of "the crumbs which fall from the master's table."
   E. Far enough to answer her prayer, "Have mercy on me, Lord, thou Son of David."

II. **Whom Can He Trust With Such?**
   A. One who is in agreement with Christ.
   B. One whose soul is occupied with proper desires.
   C. One who has faith enough to believe that He will answer distinct requests.
   D. One who can see Him in His true greatness and official capacity.
   E. One whose purpose is God's glory only.
   F. One who asks only for "the children's bread" without making selfish requests.

III. **How Shall It Be Used?**
   A. On the thing for which we have been praying most.
   B. On the salvation of souls before other things.
   C. On our children, friends and others near our hearts.
   D. On the advancement of His kingdom.

IV. **What Are It's Implications?**
   A. The mother who has faith is promised Christ's reward.
   B. Those who love the Lord ought to be like this mother.

-Adapted from C. H. Spurgeon

# The Father and the Family

*"As for me and my house, we will serve the Lord." Joshua 24:15*

## Introduction:
In most cases, it is the spiritual leadership of the father which determines the direction in which the family will move spiritually — and this is Scriptural. What a responsibility rests upon the father for the spiritual as well as the physical welfare of the family! It is his leadership under which —

### I. The Family Worships
A. What a blessing when an entire family worships together - in the church and in the home.
B. If a father is remiss in his responsibility in either area, he will reap sorrow and sadness later on.
C. When Christ is allowed to be Head of a home in all phases of its conduct, fathers will find problems of guidance lessened.

### II. The Family Loves
A. Love can be the difference between an infant's normal physical progress and slow progress. This has been proven in hospitals where babies have been kept for various reasons, and it has been noted that their progress has been slower, despite clinical conditions of food and other care, than the progress made by slum children who had poor care but mother love.
B. Love is vitally important in a child's upbringing and this the father as well as the mother can provide.

### III. The Family Learns
A. Children as well as parents learn valuable lessons in getting along together through experience.
B. The father is a learner also, but in most cases he is a teacher by example and precept.
C. Family sharing times are important.
D. Family fun together is important.

## IV. The Family Prays

A. Grace at the table is not sufficient time spent in prayer.

B. A time for family devotions together is vital to spiritual growth of all.

C. Christianity is a fellowship as well as being a way of life, and the family unit is the most basic part of this fellowship.

## V. The Family Plans

A. The time when father was the dictatorial head of the home has passed. Today a democratic atmosphere should permeate the Christian home.

B. Much of the fun of family activities lies in planning things together.

C. The same togetherness should characterize the financial aspects of family life.

## Application:

All of these aspects of family life lie in the power of the father to utilize or smother. In a very real sense, family happiness rests in the hands of the father. He is the one who speaks for his family, "As for me and my house, we will serve the Lord."

# Our Debt to our Fathers

*"Render, therefore, to all their dues. . . . " Romans 13:7*

**Introduction:**

It behooves all to render honor to whom honor is due — and to whom should we render greater honor than to our fathers? Why? Because we owe them more than any other living person. It is they who have provided for our every physical need from our earliest days. What do we owe our fathers?

I.  **Our Very Lives**
    A. Not only was our father responsible for bringing us into the world, he has also sustained our earthly lives by the labor of his hands, etc.
    B. As the head of the home, the father has also wisely led in the conduct of our very lives.

II. **Much That We Have Learned In Life**
    A. At his feet we have learned obedience.
    B. At his example we have learned to pray.
    C. From his life we have learned unselfishness and consideration for others.

III. **Our Homes**
    A. A child's greatest source of security is the home.
    B. To a great extent in this day, the father is responsible for the atmosphere if not the actual upkeep of the home.
    C. It is the father's consistent giving of himself that results in happy home-life.

IV. **Our Love In Return For His Love**
    A. Love is the greatest lesson our fathers have taught us.
    B. Love is the deepest reservoir from which we as children can draw.
    C. Our love for those around us should be a reflection of the love we have learned in the home.

## V. The Discharge Of Our Debt
A. It can never be fully repaid, but we can spend our lives being the kind of men and women our fathers would want us to be.
B. We can also show our fathers by our actions toward them and toward others that we love them and are proud of them.

**Application:**

All that has been said here about fathers is equally true of mothers and is by no means meant to minimize the important role the mother plays in the home.

LABOR DAY

# *Work as a Means of Grace*

*"And because he was of the same craft, he abode with them and wrought, for by occupation they were tentmakers."*
*Acts 18:3*

**Introduction:**
Among the Jews in early times, it was customary to teach all one's children the full details of some useful calling. It is recorded as a saying of one of the wisest Rabbis, "He who would not bring his son to a trade was as if he forced him to be a thief."

Christ's disciples were working men. Christ Himself was a carpenter. Here we see that Paul was a tentmaker. Thus we see that work is honorable. It may be and usually is wholesome for us.

Let us learn some lessons from the work of Paul.

I. **Paul's Conduct As A Worker**
   A. Paul chose a decent and reputable calling. No one can doubt that tent-making was above reproach as a business. Some occupations today are neither decent nor honorable and should not be considered by the child of God.
   B. Paul sought consistent companionship in his business. Aquila and Priscilla were intelligent, high-mind ,companionable to the man of God. Bad companions and ill-mated partners have wrecked many a business.
   C. Paul found opportunities to do good even when hardest at work. Probably he used his work as the means of the conversion of Aquila and Priscilla, and we know that they later became so spiritually knowledgable that Paul later sent Apollos to them for instruction before he began a preaching ministry.

II. **Paul's Advantages As A Worker**
   A. It put him alongside people and in sympathy with them.

B.  This contact enabled Paul to appreciate needs and discern the means of meeting them. We must realize that it is not always the fault of the poor that they do not get along well; many of them simply do not know how. They can be taught and helped by those who will take the time and effort necessary to learn and appreciate their needs.

C.  Paul's work in Corinth evidently brought cure for the despondency he was suffering when he went there. Work is often wholesome for an individual. It is also wholesome for a church; there is nothing like exercise to keep a people warm and well.

D.  Paul's work deepened his personal love for Christ. This was because he did his business for Christ and in His name. Business is a means of grace when the underlying motive for doing is love for Christ and the purpose to do His will in the spot in which He has placed us. "Prayer and provender hinder no man's journey."

-Hallock

# God's Law of Labor

*"In the sweat of thy face shalt thou eat bread,"* Genesis 3:19

**Introduction:**

Immediately after the fall of man this command was given of God for the conduct of life. Whether this was precept or a penalty is not germane to our thought today. The important thing is that it is applicable for today just as it was for Adam and Eve in their day. Notice several things:

I. **The Universality Of Labor**
   A. Adam, the "federal head" or representative of mankind, received the command, and it is passed on to all of us who have followed in his train.
   B. No one is exempt from the ruling for one exemption would nullify the entire ruling.

II. **The Need Of Labor**
   A. Without food, the fruit of our labor, all life would cease.
   B. All must do some form of labor to earn the necessities of life or be branded a parasite or a robber.

III. **The Dignity Of Labor**
   A. It is an act of worship toward God when done in the right spirit.
   B. In all too many cases, it has become an act of mere material gain.
   C. Labor is degrading only when performed from wrong motives or when its fruit is dishonoring to God.

IV. **The Reward Of Labor**
   A. To eat is to live; existence is the reward of labor.
   B. Every man has the right to this much, but no man has the right to expect more as a matter of course (Job 1:21; I Timothy 6:7 & 8).
   C. Having food and clothing, we should be content.

# V. The Equality Of Labor

A. All are alike in God's sight for He is no respecter of persons.

B. This does not mean that there is no place for employer and employee for each has his function to perform and should do it to the best of his ability..

# *All in a Day's Work*

*Ephesians 6:5-8; Colossians 3:23*

**Introduction:**
It is interesting to watch people work. So often they are so very unlike. One will be dilligent and seem to enjoy work thoroughly. Another will be desultory and seem to despise the whole business. The way in which we face our work responsibilities is very important for us as Christians.

**I. The Rut Of The Routine**
    A. We are caught in the "sameness" of our daily tasks.
    B. This leads to a "loss of significance" in relationship to the task. Our job then becomes just "another job" or simply a means of making a living.
    C. This results in some familiar problems.
        1. The "trapped" feeling.
        2. The person who is over-worked.
        3. Excessive changes of jobs.
        4. Nervous and emotional problems.

**II. The Recommended Reversal**
    A. We must realize the Scriptural theme.
        1. "Whatsoever ye do, do it heartily as unto the Lord."
        2. Covers the entire spectrum of the whole of life.
    B. We must see our work as "unto the Lord."
    C. We must reorganize our lives around this theme.

**III. The Resultant Renewal**
    A. Our "job" will take on new significance.
    B. Our whole outlook toward life may be changed.
    C. The new outlook will permeate all areas of life.
    D. More work gets done, and all of it is "to the glory of God."

# *Thanksgiving Day*

*". . .for this day is holy unto our Lord. . . ." Nehemiah 8:9&10*

**Introduction:**
The Scripture records an early Thanksgiving day which began with solemnity and ended in joy. Let us look at it and see what we can learn concerning the spirit of thanksgiving.

I.  **Profound Meditation Precedes True Thankfulness**
Our thankfulness must reach down to plumb depths of spiritual reality if it is truly to rise to the greatest heights of joy.

II. **Thanksgiving Need Not Be Postponed Until All Is Perfect**
It must discern the divine plan; it need not be dependent upon the surrounding circumstances. Someone has said, "You will have as much material prosperity as is good for you in most cases."

III. **Thanksgiving Brings Joy As We Share Our Blessings**
We do this through various means:
A. Our worship in the church.
B. Through our spreading of the Gospel to others.
C. Through our moving to meet the needs of those around us.

# *Thanksgiving to the Father*

*"Giving thanks unto the Father, which hath made us meet to be partakers of the inheritance of the saints in light: who hath delivered us . . . into the kingdom of his dear Son."*
*Colossians 1:12 & 13*

**Introduction:**
Such a section of Scripture as this makes us aware of all the blessings and benefits which accrue to us because of the Father's blessing. Look at several aspects of God's blessing.

I.  **His Blessings Look Backward**
    A.  We can recall what we once were.
        1.  Under the power of spiritual and moral darkness.
        2.  Under the discipline of darkness.
    B.  We are now in the marvelous light of His glory.

II.  **His Blessings Look Forward**
    A.  The true believer is fit for eternal life in heaven.
        1.  Heaven is an inheritance which sons will receive.
        2.  Heaven is an inheritance which saints will receive.
    B.  We look to the future for the absolute completion of our salvation.

III.  **His Blessings Are For The Present**
    A.  We are right now blessed "with all spiritual blessings in heavenly places in Christ."
    B.  We have the glory of knowing the presence of the Lord day by day.

IV.  **His Blessings Are Cause For Thanksgiving**
Without Christ, one is weak and helpless. How thankful we should be for all that is provided us in Him — both for eternity and also for time. At this time of the year we are often guilty of limiting ourselves to thanking God for the material blessings to the exclusion of the Spiritual. We ought to turn our attention to the gifts of God, "with whom there is no variableness neither shadow cast by turning."

-Adapted from C. H. Spurgeon

## Gratitude for God's Remembrances

*"How precious also are thy thoughts unto me, O God."*
*Psalms 139:17*

**Introduction:**
The sense of loneliness is always saddening. In such an hour how consoling to feel that we are remembered by at least one human being. How much more consoling to know that we are thought of with loving interest by a goodly number of friends. Yet what are either of these assurances to the supreme consciousness that God remembers us and that we share in His benevolent plans.

I. **His Thoughts Of Us Are Loving Thoughts**
   He is our Father and lovingly thoughtful of all His dear children.

II. **His Thoughts Of Us Are Constant Thoughts**
   He simply never forgets. In all places, times and circumstances, he thinks of us constantly.

III. **His Thoughts Of Us Are Personal Thoughts**
   He does not think of us as indefinable parts of some indefinite multitude.

IV. **His Thoughts Of Us Are Wise Thoughts**
   His plans for us are the best possible plans.

V. **His Thoughts Of Us Are Helpful Thoughts**
   We may think of a person without any disposition or desire to help him. But God has the disposition and willingness to help and thinks on us with the purpose of helping ever in mind.

# *Loaded with Benefits*

*"Blessed be the Lord, who daily loadeth us with benefits, even the God of our salvation." Psalm 68:19*

**Introduction:**
At a time of Thanksgiving, the child of God must reflect on the abundant blessings which are his because he is a child of God and thus is part of a special relationship existing between God and His children.

I. **The Nature Of This Relationship**
   A. The plan of salvation was made by God.
   B. The work of salvation was carried out by God.
   C. The blessings of salvation are applied by God.
   D. The final outcome of salvation is the result of God.

II. **The Benefits Of This Relationship**
   A. Their nature or quality.
   B. Their number or quantity.
   C. Their frequency

III. **The Demands Of This Relationship**
   A. We should live for Him sincerely.
   B. We should live for Him affectionately.
   C. We should live for Him constantly and consistently.
   D. We should live for Him practically.

# *Thanksgiving*

*"Abounding . . . in Thanksgiving . . ." Colossians 2:7*

**Introduction:**
Sometimes it is not easy for us to see the import of such admonitions as this. But there are some things about thanksgiving that we would do well to mark.

I. **Thanksgiving Is A Duty**
If this seems unacceptable, read the text and see Colossians 3:15ff.

II. **Thanksgiving Is A Privilege**
Actually we are fortunate to be so constructed that we can enjoy things enough to want to express our thanksgiving.

III. **Thanksgiving Should Be Continuous**
Every day should be a "Thanksgiving Day" rather than one special day being set apart for this function once each year.

IV. **Thanksgiving Should Have A Prominent Part** In Life
This is especially true in the case of the child of God. "Abounding in thanksgiving."

V. **Thanksgiving Should Recognize The Spiritual**
We are tempted to become very much minded with the material things which we have. Actually, spiritual gifts are of supreme importance.

## *Back to Work with Joy*

*"And the shepherds returned, glorifying and praising God for all the things that they had heard and seen, as it was told unto them." Luke 2:20*

**Introduction:**
The shepherds had just seen angels, heard their marvelous music, had seen the Christ. After that experience we read that they "returned." With joy they returned to their common duty, back to their sheep.

The difference between Christian joy and the world's pleasure is in this: the one fits for duty, while the other unfits. Three thoughts are suggested in this.

**I. Christ Brings Joy**
That angels sang when Christ was born. Simeon and Anna returned thanks. Andrew shouted "Eureka." A man may rejoice indeed when he finds the Saviour.

**II. Christ Brings Joy Into The Performance Of Duty**
The shepherds went back to work gladly. Christ brought the disciples down from the mountain to where the demoniac child was. Paul exhorts Christians to live contentedly where they are. Onesimus was sent back to his earthly master. Our joy in Christ is to fit us for the every-day duties.

**III. Christ Would Have Gratitude Expressed In Work**
The best way to praise God is by our lives. There is not much spirituality in the man who won't work. The birds praise God by their songs, the flowers by their beauty, the stars by their shining and their motion in their spheres. We can best "adorn the doctrine" and praise God by our lives.

# The Son of Man is Come

*"The Son of Man is come to seek and to save that which was lost." Luke 19:10*

**Introduction:**
This splendid verse provides a tremendous wealth of information in the very words which it contains. Let us consider them:

**I.   The Son Of Man**
He is the "Wonderful, Counselor, Mighty God. . . ." Out of love for a fallen race He lays aside His glory and becomes the Son of Man (by the very term stressing the humanity into which He entered). This is the title which the Lord appropriates to Himself.

**II.  Is Come**
He was not forced or compelled, but He came of His own volition. This statement also stresses an historical fact which must be reckoned with.

**III. To Seek**
It is interesting to observe in the life of Christ how often He sought for the souls of men and was engaged in ministering to them.

**IV. To Save**
He came because there was something precious to save, something which had infinite worth in His sight.

**V.   That Which Was Lost**
Lays stress on the fact that man was lost without Him. It speaks of the sin which He came to combat and defeat.

# The Wise Men's Quest for a King

*"There came wise men from the east . . . saying, Where is he that is born King of the Jews?" Matthew 2:1, 2*

**Introduction:**
As one considers this verse and this story from the earthly life of Christ, four questions come to mind which must be asked and answered.

**I.   Who Were The Seekers?**
They came from afar, representing the best among the Gentiles, the noblest among men all over the world. They had possibly been influenced by the great religious leader, Zoroaster. He led a movement which worshiped a strange and unseen Light and thought of God as an infinite Spirit. Followers of this philosophy led exemplary lives, believing in prayer, judgment and immortality. Yet these men, good as they were, realized that they needed something more.

**II.  What Did They Seek?**
They were looking for a King. They realized that a man needs someone to rule him for he cannot rule himself. He needs someone wiser than he is to direct him. Spiritually, man needs a king just as he needs some organized form of political government. These wise men, then, were looking for a King to whom they could wisely pledge their allegiance. We, too, need a spiritual foundation on which to build, a King whom we can follow.

**III. How Did They Find Him?**
They followed the only knowledge they had — a wisdom gained from many years studying the stars. And a star led them to their King. He was their supreme desire, the One they wanted above all else. We, too, must desire Him above all else, and act according to the light he grants us. The wise men found Him by following the star, the shepherds while guarding their flocks.

## IV. Where Did They Find Him?

The Highest had revealed Himself in the lowliest — God was found in the form of a Babe. He still comes to us in this form. He comes to us where we are. He does not expect us to raise ourselves to His level before we can find Him.

## V. What Did They Do After They Had Found Him?

They gave Him the best that they had. Down through the centuries the cream of thinkers, of scientists, have been men of God. These men not only gave of the best that they *had*, but they gave of *themselves* as individuals to serve Him. Just so, we must give Him ourselves. Jesus was born in Bethlehem, and He is born again, as it were, into every heart that will receive Him.

CHRISTMAS

# *The Unspeakable Gift*

*"Thanks be unto God for his unspeakable gift." II Cor. 9:15*

**Introduction:**
The gifts of God are absolutely incomparable. There is such a greatness in them that Paul was forced to coin an inexpressible expression in order to communicate in any way the glory of God's gifts.

Towering above all His other gifts, however, is the gift of His Son.

**I. It Is The Best Gift**
The heart yearns for love, and in this gift we see love at its ultimate. "Greater love hath no man than this. . ." "Herein is love, not that we loved God, but that God loved us. . ." "For God so loved the world. . ."

**II. It Includes All Other Gifts**
If you have Christ, you have the key to any and all the gifts which God gives to men. "How shall He not with Him freely give us all things?"

**III. It Is The Gift Which Improves All Other Gifts**
The presence of one possession may add to the worth of all others. This is true with the gift of Christ; all seems better for it.
A. We value nature more.
B. We value human nature more.
C. We value the Bible more.

**IV. It Is The Gift Which Makes Us Givers**
When we receive it, we become like it and seek to share it with others.

**V. It Is A Gift Given To All People**
A. Note that it is a gift and not a loan.
B. It is a gift and not a purchase.
C. It is a gift which draws forth thanks.
    1. By the giving of gifts to others.
    2. By giving ourselves to the giver.
—Adapted

## The Last Sermon of the Year

*"Give an account of thy stewardship; for thou mayest be no longer steward." Luke 16:2*

**Introduction:**
At the close of the year, it is a good time to give some thought to the possibility that we might be removed from the place of responsibility in the things of life in the year ahead.

I. **It Is A Reasonable Demand**
   A. If you have done wrong, it is best to catch it right at this moment and make correction.
   B. Making an accounting now will help you to prize your salvation and your Saviour that much more.
   C. It might bring the unsaved person to face his problems right at this point.

II. **It Is A Comprehensive Demand**
   A. Give an account of:
      1. Your stewardship. 2. Your talents. 3. Your substance and your use of it. 4. Your time. 5. Your influence. 6. Your responsibility.
   B. It is an accounting to God that is demanded. We have responsibility to others, but we do not have to give them an accounting.
   C. We have interest in others, but we will not have to answer for what they have done but only for our own lives.

III. **It Is An Urgent Demand**
   A. One's stewardship could be lost through loss of life, health, etc.
   B. One's stewardship could be lost through loss of opportunity for service.
   C. The old year, with its triumphs and mistakes, is past. A new year awaits you — is at your disposal to do with as you see fit — to be used for God or frittered away on non-essentials. What will you do with it?

-Adapted from C. H. Spurgeon